Canadian Wild Animals

Canadian Wild Animals

Copyright © 1994 by Colleayn O. Mastin

Canadian Cataloguing in Publication Data

Mastin, Colleayn, O. (Colleayn Olive)
    Canadian Wild Animals

Nature Canada Series; 1
    ISBN 1-895910-00-5 (bound). -- ISBN
    1-895910-03-x (pbk.)
    1. Zoology--Canada--Juvenile literature.
    I. Sovak, Jan,1953-   II. Title.   III. Series.
    QL721.M38 1994   j591.971
    C93-091872-X

PUBLISHED BY ~

GRASSHOPPER BOOKS
106 - WADDINGTON DRIVE
KAMLOOPS, BRITISH COLUMBIA
CANADA V2E 1M2

A portion of the sales
of this book will be
donated to the
Canadian Nature Federation

This book is dedicated to Adam, Blair, Robert, Brock, Jackson, Bradley, Brenden, Codi, Kurt, Jesse, Tyson, Joel and Aaron.

Acknowledgement

The author wishes to thank the following individuals for their contributions to this book ~ Jack and Iris Stout, Dennis Johnson, Kelly Meston, Michelle Locken, Heather-Faye Mastin, Idella Forfylow, Don Swan, Michele Thornley, Joy Reynoldson, Mary Lilburn, Pamela Holden, Jann Bailey, Evelyn Hoffman, Josh Lockwood, Dan Holden, Shirley Roth.

DESIGN & PRODUCTION BY ~ BLACKBIRD DESIGN, CALGARY, ALBERTA
PRINTED IN CANADA BY ~ FRIESEN PRINTERS LTD., ALTONA, MANITOBA

Beaver

Beavers are their busiest,
When their forest world is dark;
They're skilled at cutting trees down;
Their favourite food is bark.

Beavers
wonderful buil
With their huge front t
that keep growing all the t
they can bite through small t
and then carry them to a stream. There they build a stick-
mud dam, and a lodge which is their ho

Beaver babies are called kits, and they stay with their parents for two ye
Then they are sent off to form their own colonies. Beavers have a broad
tail. If danger is near, they slap their tail on the water to warn other beav

When the beaver eats its favourite food, the bark of trees, it rolls a
branch in its front paws, in much the same way that people eat a cob of c

Beavers mate for life. The beaver is the national animal emblem of Car
and is North America's largest rod

avers live in families,

d none can sit and dream,

nile the others "work like beavers",

dam a pond or stream.

Bear

There are two kinds of bears,
One a grizzly, one a black;
The grizzly is much bigger
With a large hump on its back.

Bears aren't fussy eaters,
They like both meat and plants.
They're especially fond of berries,
And salmon, honey and ants.

During her long, cold winter sleep, one or two cubs are born to the mother bear, who is called a sow. Mother bears protect their cubs fiercely and stay with the cubs through their second winter. After the cubs are born, the mother bear stays away from adult males, as they have been known to kill the young cubs.

The den of a bear may be under a tree stump or a hole in a hillside. Female bears usually line their dens with grass, ferns or leaves, so it is comfortable and cozy for the cubs. Males usually do not make their dens so comfortable.

Black bears have fur that is coloured brown, cinnamon, white or black. The colour of a grizzly can range from white to ivory or from black to brown.

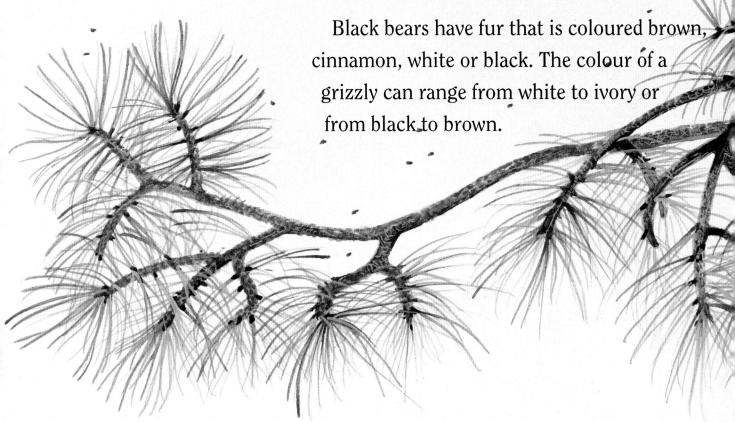

The killing of the
buffalo began almost one hundred an
fifty years ago. Where once there were
vast herds of buffalo, fewer than one
thousand animals were left alive.

Today, several thousand buffalo are protected in a number c
national parks located in western Canada.

Buffalo are herbivorous. This means that they eat various types of grasses,
vines and lichens. In the winter they search for food by clearing away the snow
with their strong front hooves and massive head.

Buffalo cows give birth to a single calf in the spring.
Both the male and female buffalo look after the calf.

uffalo

e largest prairie mammal
alled the buffalo;
t herds roamed our prairies,
t very long ago.

But humans came to hunt them,
By the millions they were slain;
We protect them now in buffalo parks,
And the herds grow strong again.

Coyote

The coyote is a wild dog,
Hills and prairies are its home;
It's like a wolf, except that—
It likes to hunt alone.

Since they are dogs, coyotes
In daytime like to growl;
But when the moon is shining,
They really like to howl.

Coyotes are bigger than foxes, but smaller than wolves. They live on the [pra]iries, in open woodlands or in brushy, rocky areas.

In the evening, they make high-pitched yelping sounds, then a long howl [tha]t ends in short sharp yips. These sounds can be especially scary to [cam]pers sleeping in a tent under the stars.

Coyotes will eat almost anything but, are most fond of rabbits, squirrels, [mic]e, eggs and insects. They also eat berries and some fruits.

Each spring, five to seven pups are born. Male coyotes are very good fathers and do their share in looking after the young pups.

Deer

Most deer live in forests
Since they're secretive and shy;
But some are found in city parks
Where people live nearby.

The big ones are the buck and doe,
The baby is the fawn;
If this family senses danger,
Suddenly it's gone!

Spotted, wobbly-legged fawns are born in late spring. Usually the doe has twins and these newborn fawns get to their feet within minutes. During the first two weeks, the doe leaves them in a hiding spot but returns often to feed them.

The fawns have very little smell. This, combined with their spotted coats, which act as a camouflage, help to protect them from coyotes, wolves, lynx and bobcats.

When they grow bigger, they run in short dashes, bounds or leaps. Deer nibble twigs, shrubs, fungi, acorns, grass and herbs.

Fox

In many stories, foxes
Are said to be quite sly,
Though really foxes are just smart
And very, very shy.

Foxes like to hunt at night
Then den up in the day;
Their fur is red or brown or white,
Or sometimes silver-gray.

When the pups are about one month old, they are big enough to leave the den and what fun they have! Outside, they sniff, jump, play with twigs or rocks, and chase butterflies and feathers. This play helps them to become good hunters.

After the pups are born, the mother called a vixen, stays safely hidden in the den with her litter of three to five pups. This den can be a spot in the hollow of a tree, a space between rocks or even a hole in the ground.

The father hunts and carries birds, squirrels and other food back to the family. As the pups get stronger, both parents teach them to pounce on mice, rabbits and frogs and how to search for eggs, insects and fruit.

When fall arrives, the mother forces the pups out of the den for they must now leave to find a mate and raise families of their own.

Mountain Goat

Mountain goats are walkers,
They don't much like to run;
What they really like is climbing
Up a mountain in the sun.

Mountain goats in winter,
Have coats of snowy white;
In summer, when their shedding,
They're a most repulsive sight.

Mountain goats spend most of the year moving about in small groups, called flocks. In the summertime, they graze in the meadows above the timberline. During the winter, they come down to the lower levels. There, they find grasses and plants on the mountain faces that are too steep to hold snow.

Their enemies are bears, cougars, wolves and coyotes. They can defend themselves against these enemies by moving easily across mountain slopes where these animals cannot follow.

Each year in the spring, the mother, has one kid, although sometimes there are twins. Both the female and male goats have sharp slightly curved black horns.

You can tell the age of a mountain goat by counting the rings on its horn and adding one year.

Groundhog

On February second,

The groundhog wakes from sleep,

Then leaves its den and steps outside

To give the sky a peep.

If the sky is cloudy,

No shadows on the ground,

It thinks, "Ah, winter's over,

I think I'll stick around".

But if the sky is cloudy,

And cold and blue and deep,

It dives back in its burrow,

For six more weeks of sleep.

Groundhogs are like digging machines and can bury themselves out of sight as quick as a wink! These fat furry creatures are members of the squirrel family.

During the winter, they hibernate for several months in their warm cozy burrows under the ground. Sometimes they get restless and stir about. They usually end their long sleep in early March.

Then, when it is warm, they come out and start nibbling and eating green grasses, clover, plants and sometimes corn.

Should one of their enemies, such as a fox, lynx or coyote come snooping around, they signal danger by making shrill calls to warn other groundhogs. Groundhogs are also called "woodchucks".

The Canada lynx hunts rabbits at night in the deep forest where it lives. Its favourite food is rabbit, but if it is not quick enough to catch one, it will settle for rodents, squirrels, birds or a tasty fox.

In winter, the lynx grows heavy fur on the top and bottom of its big feet. These furry feet act like snowshoes that keep the lynx from sinking into the deep soft snow when it is hunting.

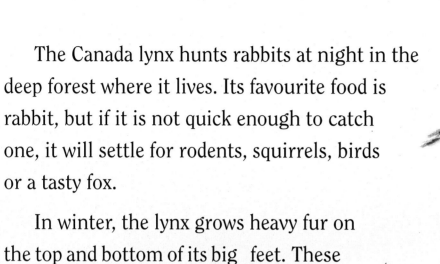

Each spring the mother lynx has a litter of four to six kittens which she looks after all by herself. Usually a lynx kills every other night and eats about one hundred and fifty to two hundred rabbits each year.

Canada Lynx

A lynx looks like your cat
Though it has much bigger feet;
Rabbits, hares and field mice
Are what it likes to eat.

It sort of makes you wonder
What Nature had in mind,
When she gave the lynx such different ears
And a short tail out behind.

A moose's body is thick and wide,
With stilt-like legs below;
These help a moose in winter-time
To wander through deep snow.

A mother moose gives birth to twins
In June or late in May;
And when these calves are one year old,
She sends them on their way.

Moose

The calf is helpless at birth, so the mother moose, called a cow, hides it in the bush away from its enemies—bears, wolves and wolverine.

The voice of a newborn calf is a low grunt but after a few days, it develops a wail that sounds just like a human baby.

Moose eat twigs and shrubs. They also like water plants and sometimes dive six metres down to a lake bottom for this tasty food.

The fur-covered skin that hangs from its throat is called a bell. The moose is the largest of the deer family. In spite of its great size, it can move almost as silently as a cat through dense forest.

Otters

River otters love to play,
Especially in the water,
When sliding down a muddy bank,
They're doing what they "otter".

River otters catch small fish
On which they like to snack;
They prefer to eat their dinner,
While floating on their back.

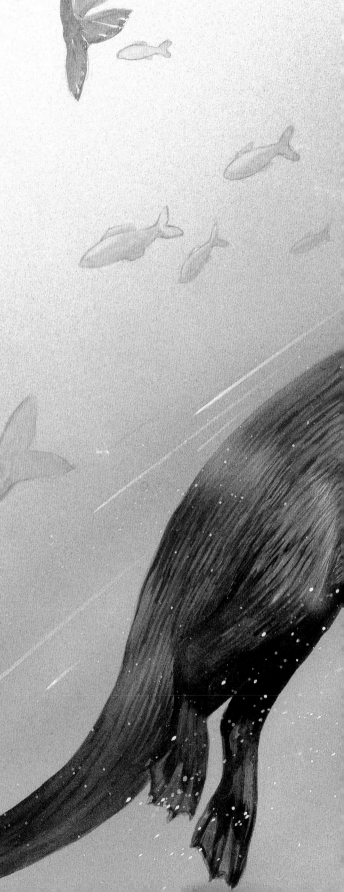

It is fun to watch otters at play. They will
slide and tumble down the steep banks of
streams or lakes into the water, looking just like
children tobogganing down a snowy slope.

River otters are the smartest of all the weasel
family. They dig their dens along the river banks
with the entrances below the water. This way, the
otters can dive into the water, slip into their dens, and
escape from their enemies.

Otters are swift and skilful swimmers. They can easily catch the
h, frogs, crayfish and other water animals that are their food.

A mother otter gives birth to one to five babies in the spring. The young
rs stay with their mother for nearly a year. She teaches them to swim and
, to lie quietly or dive when danger is near.

Porcupine

The very prickly porcupine
Is great at climbing trees,
Though on the ground, it moves as if
It's running on its knees.

For its defence, the porcupine
Has quills each like a pin,
If it slaps a creature with its tail,
It won't come near again!

The porcupine
can afford to be brave. It wears a
suit of 30,000 sharp, barbed quills.

It moves clumsily through the forest, usually
at night. During the day it can often be seen hunched
into a large, black ball in a tree.

When an enemy comes close, the porcupine turns its
back and lashes its tail to one side. The quills will then stick into
any nearby paw, face or foot. An experienced hunter, such as the wolf,
will roll the porcupine on its back and then kill it.

Porcupines eat bark, buds and the leaves of trees. They also like salt and
many of them get killed trying to lick up the salt used to melt snow on the
highways. The female porcupine gives birth to only one baby each spring.

Rabbit

The soft and furry rabbit
Likes to feed at night,
Avoiding hungry owls,
By keeping out of sight!

This long-legged rabbit
Can speed off in high gear;
And many, many rabbits
Join the family every year.

A rabbit must be very careful not to become a dinner for one of its many enemies—the fox, owl, and coyote. Its brownish summer fur turns white in winter, but its fluffy tail is always white and looks like a powder puff.

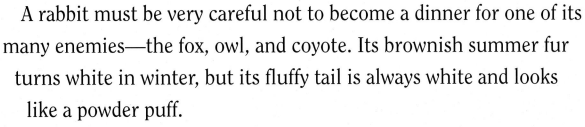

During the day, the rabbit sits safely in its lair. At night, it comes out to feed on grasses and other plants. In the winter, it tunnels in the snow to keep warm.

A mother rabbit can give birth to as many as twenty five babies each year.

When frightened, rabbits thump the ground with a back leg to warn nearby rabbits. The doe or female rabbit is larger than the male rabbit, which is called a buck.

Raccoon

Raccoons look like burglars,
With that mask across their face;
All day they sleep, but in the night,
They steal from place to place.

Perhaps you own a panda bear,
A stuffed one, and quite tame;
You can tell these two are cousins,
Their faces look the same.

Most raccoons live in the forest but some live in cities. These city raccoons look for food in garbage cans or in people's gardens. Raccoons have adapted to city living better than most wild animals.

They can use their paws like hands, and are excellent climbers. Raccoons have an interesting habit of playing with their food in water before eating it. Night-time is when raccoons usually search for their meals. They eat crayfish, birds' eggs, fruit and nuts. Their favourite food is corn.

A raccoon's home is usually a den in the hollow of a tree, a log or a burrow in the ground. Raccoons are found in every part of Canada except Newfoundland.

Skunk

The creatures we call skunks
Are famous for their smell;
And all across this country
These little stinkers dwell.

They are black and white and furry,
Just as cuddly as can be,
But if by chance you get too close,
PHEW-EE!